Dewy Decimal

First published 2020 by The Hedgehog Poetry Press

Published in the UK by
The Hedgehog Poetry Press
5, Coppack House
Churchill Avenue
Clevedon
BS21 6QW

www.hedgehogpress.co.uk

ISBN: 978-1-9160908-8-0

9 8 7 6 5 4 3 2 1

A CIP Catalogue record for this book is available from the
British Library.

Contents

Dewy Decimal

by

Kristin Garth

Prisons have libraries -- even yours, a Florida panhandle two story with unlockable doors, half-brick, half-aluminum siding — no concrete, barbed wire, even a privacy fence to enclose adolescent desires, too afraid to evince. Its warden/patriarch adequately prevents insurrections with temper and belt, teenage girl fears (being tortured and felt, as you have been for years in a cage staged like a bedroom; confined in his rage, designed like a tomb). All this plus his prohibition to earn a wage, to date or learn how to drive deprives you of mobility, keeps you inside.

You flee only to the humidity, to teal tufts, sporadic, in sandy soil you call yard until its dry tickle recalls other prickles — the hard you discard, but the soft always sticks, salt and peppered male patterned baldness against a shivered inside of thigh. You can't make it leave you no matter how hard you —

Try, wet eyes, to breathe and focus on just one printed word — not necessarily the next just the text, least blurred, below a chin, against your breasts. Lying on your stomach in your bed or in this half-ass grass, always rests a book. Inside of pages are places, exotic escapes from a cul de sac of horrors decorated demure. Prisons have libraries, yes, even yours.

HOT PINK

Hot pink hydrangea tomb teenage, a cell
of swallowed bubblegum and rage. A door
I cannot lock to hide. A car they will
not allow me to drive. I'm stuck indoors
and in my head, but Henry Miller's in
my bed, abreast of Faulkner, Tennessee —
write harlots, captives, sad, like me. Girl friend
in ink Joyce Carol Oates, empathy,
erotic anecdotes. Next year eighteen,
if I survive, hot pink, full bloomed but half
alive. I do my time with the Marquis
de Sade. He sees my jailhouse virtue, laughs
"you fraud." Compatriots in sheets hot pink,
you wet your prison blossom, on the brink.

The word might have been Nembutal. All these years later, impossible to
recall — perhaps it was gurney or coroner or lividity. It could have been
something innocuous as yellow or the. Something morbid, technical, equally
likely, because your suburban prison library is sublimely curated by a morbid
Mormon mother obsessed with true crime.

It might have been a book about Marilyn — had lots of them, much
discussion of her skin, but not ones where she's ambulatory, arching or even
alive. She's on some man's table, a corpse in perpetuity exposed. He didn't
need scissors to cut off her clothes, Noguchi — the coroner who eviscerates
stars then recalls each experience in best selling memoirs. Your mother
collects their autopsies, details of celebrity demise. Some have R-rated
movies she can't see because the prophet decries, but their murders are
fitting for Puritan eyes.

You pick up these tomes and they become part of who you are, a girl who
reads autopsies on the way home from church in the car. You have clues,
Agatha Christies, Nancy Drews, a rainbow collection of approved youth
literature spines (your favorite, Wuthering Heights), but true crimes and
dissected bodies sleep next to you most hot southern nights.

CLUES

A girl detective, River Heights, as keen
on lockets, pearls as legal rights. You're robbed
a mother, three year's old. This jinx, a teen,
deciphers — never told. A turning knob
reveals a mystery. All they won't tell,
by candlelight you see. You speak in French
but not of loss. A roadster, blue pastel,
to house of moss. A missing clock, suspense —
what does it hide? Bank box details you find
inside. Accept no money for a case,
your pride, their pleasure a reward entwined,
that spider sapphire, rare, you can't replace.
A staircase secret seen through eyes ice blue;
in lilac, step through strife, collect your clues.

Your education of bodies begins with the wrong — disembowelment, rape,
buttoned-up-to-the-neck pajamas, long. Some of it's read on shag closet
floors, nude, by flashlight. Some you'll dread, unlocked doors, in bedsheets
that smell, even clean, of undetectable sweat, perpetual fright. You learn,
alone, with your fingers, how to be gentle and light.

Each touch erases a memory you don't want to see. You want to know more
— to learn how to be. You can't watch the Facts of Life or movies R-rated,
but they don't censor books with contents covered, discreetly illustrated. It's
literature they know nothing about — the church has made no proclamations
to parents devout. You are ignorant of pleasure, educated in pain. The
former's not something Mormons believe or explain.

But they've been driving you somewhere to learn since you're three. You're
sure you could find pleasure, yourself, inside a library.

LIBRARY WINDOW SEAT

Climb into a man-made moon. Curved seat,
perched feet, pockmarked plastic bubble cocoon,
bruised, Big Blue Marble Atlas, trick or treat
concrete, you muse escape, June afternoons,

discrete. Crepe homemade dress against wall-star-
brush-stroked sky, booking your first alibi,
you hover over a glass door ajar
while daddy wonders where you are –

above spines, pages, patrons, mystery
of limbs, pulled hems (hope he won't see); clench shut
eyes, thighs. Become a continent with seas
and natural boundaries none abut

until you are found, pulled down, always too soon
by gravity stronger than plastics moons.

Ms. Rose knows a book you will like from the look of an eye. Her voice is a whisper of wishes; you concentrate all July. You scoot closer, criss-cross applesauce, your third summertime. Must capture the cadence, her ladylike pantomime mingled with rhyme.

They call it storytime, but it is more puppet show. She tells tales twirling, tulip skirt, through a carpet of child marionettes below. She holds the books in her hand, the pictures square to young eyes. Her own never appear to touch pages, contents memorized.

Kids study, the smitten, her kitten heels with pastel pleather bows. You see the freckles inside the shimmer of nude pantyhose. She bends down reciting a passage to you, brown bob across flushed cheek/eye shadowed blue.

You hope you'll be like her some day when you're grown, emancipated by age, a place all your own, a bookish career in backseam pantyhose, voice a little angelic/assertive juxtaposed. She is who you hope to be — and Ms. Rose knows.

A LIBRARY CARD IS A LICENSE OF THE MIND

Her polka-dotted patterned calves gallop
prepubescent paths, story time, equine
imitations in kitten heels. Scalloped
peep toe library show reveals define
universality, woman you want
to be — not property in homemade dress,
cardholder in a world of yes. Type font
cardstock, signed, squeezed, tiny envelope pressed
palm to Hello Kitty purse, gift of hope,
license of the mind, proffered by paragon,
womankind, with novel geography. Scope
her catalogued cartography. Denouement,
despite father, your omnipresent guard,
she will issue you a library card.

You wear dresses to school, a Puritan rule to look like a lady even while you're
still a little girl. "Pants are for women who want to be men" (something your
father says again and again) – it's never too early for you to begin looking like
someone's future wife. It's exactly the point of your miserable, miniscule life.
So while the other girls your age wear shorts, ribbons, running shoes, you are
predestined by dress to lose – all races, be they by teacher organized, or
hormonal informal, pack of boys chasing you, part thrilled/traumatized at the
thought they will catch you and give you a kiss.

Your only chance is to find a good place to hide with another they miss, a girl,
your age, second grade, avoiding their lips – a sweaty convoy who employ the
pseudonym "the kissing boys." You listen for feet but just hear the noise of one
little girl's breath as rapid as yours. You huddle, two compatriots, in your first
tunnel trenches of a gender war.

You haven't kissed anyone ever before. Even so young, you're used to men
taking and you can't abide anymore. You want to know what it is to give to
someone you choose and adore. She's pressed up against concrete, a trembling
frame, skin against skin, a little hot and ashamed. Her hair and her breath on
your neck where they fall, prompted by the sound of male footfall outside
somewhere.

You feel her lips – maybe accident or because of these events, but you take them
and return. You're too young to even discern what any of this says about your
sexuality. All you know is you wanted it to be exactly just like this when you
received your first kiss – and though you guess you assumed it would be a boy.
You learn early, in this world of pain, to never limit joy.

INSIDE

The two you miss. My raveled ribbon yanked,
dismissed. A chase to tunnels, huddled pleas
while we hug knees. A gingham dress that flanks
a goosebumped tease of skinny arm I squeeze.

We hear your feet. They pound playground,
a pack that grows discreet but close. We hear
the menace and the squeak. So sure we're found,
our arms go round, so near we disappear.

I feel her breath. A rhythm on my neck
it beats as quick as your retreat. A brush
of lips a jaunty journey to my cheek. A peck
so soft, unsure it's real until I peek and blush.

A concrete five-foot tunnel where we hide,
escape your kiss, we make our bliss inside.

They blossom in window box on beige library shelf, black spine, white curlicue,
you pluck yourself a paper flower, red shuttered bloom of a dark-fated, related
bride & groom. It feels familiar, familial from first feather-edged page lip gloss,
hot fudge/soy sauce? – embossed, fingerprints of flower girls your own age.

Inside of its covers mocked up like a house, they hide inside attics problematic --
no mouse fed arsenic but children of sin. Cloistered together until it happens
again. They call it gothic horror, but it's nonfiction to you. You read it for
company, to know what to do –

Then you see paperback copies in rainbow-hued arms, in middle school
hallways. You feel increasingly alarmed. They paginate a particular horror
you're living through — and all these pubescent purveyors of VC Andrews
volumes, could they all be like you?

Do they hide in a closet, severed petals and pride? Do they know a soul
teleports from what it cannot abide? Do they hope they'll survive to be a woman
someday? Why the fuck did they pluck this incestuous bouquet?

FLOWER IN YOUR ATTIC

for VC Andrews & my mother

The plain are paranoid of pretty things,
not pastel kitchens, wedding rings but what
begins, pink skin, inside a pious womb then flings
libidinous limbs in living rooms. Smut

      inside dark irises, omnipotent
as even his, lewd lord of Foxworth Hall
who craves betrayal, Dresden dolls; he's meant
to suffer. Girls will pay. Wife, after all,

      never really looks away — you're well aware
of blossomed breasts, honeysuckle hair hides
sly-one-doe-eyed requests. Walk me upstairs
to whips where unmarred skin is sanctified.

You made a petaled thing he would adore.
Deflower me behind locked attic doors.

Knowledge is laundry folded in small hardwood drawers with codes made of numbers designating where it is stored. You go to her first when you're very small, and she pulls out a stool until you grow tall enough to open each drawer you never could reach. Ms. Rose will assist, but, more importantly, teach you to find all the answers no one will tell – to pull open each drawer and savor the smells of freedom and knowledge, the tulip and dirt.

She speaks in whispers, even the card stock's too used, malleable to hurt – like cotton you scribble down digits of witches, mysteries you hide in the pocket of skirts, a map to anything you want to explore. Nobody censors – calls you a whore. Life in these hours is a series of opening drawers.

You are a human with rights your fingers can find – inscribed in a volume with a number assigned. There's no part of this building Ms. Rose forbids you to see. On industrial carpet, in stacks, you read your first book on human sexuality. You know the abnormal, what's not talked about. At school, they had an assembly but you were kept out by puritans who didn't want you to know more than pain and control, the necessary horrors of the menstrual flow, the making of babies and the shutting of thighs. Sex is sadistic, a stolen virtue and lies.

But in books, you read stories of another kind – boys and girls in the woods with lascivious minds. The moaning at midnight for paragraphs, seduction in volumes, graveyards, in slang and in dialects, the language of bards. You take home a stack and reread pages before into bubbles you climb. Where you lay back against porcelain, to sensations sublime, pleasure, like knowledge, opens as easily as drawers. Your fingers remember your body is yours.

CARD CATALOVE

My Google was an opened drawer. Five
by three inch maps in oak all stored. A flip
of card stock fingered, feathered tips. Alive
with smells: vanilla, grass, lemon, tulip.

Research a person dug into, a file,
aflutter, fell while fingertips reviewed.
Aged paper smudged and smoothed by touch, tactile.
Alighted, too, the accidental, new.

Required you enter a library. Talk
to people, collect then carry. Wander
and whisper, excavate. You stalked the stacks,
climb stools and contemplate — public ponder.

Shapeshifter's exiled bones in antique stores.
Once knowledge lived its life inside a drawer.

In elementary school, you participate in some informal, extracurricular plays – on the playground, the ending of each uneventful elementary school day.   Your first director here – anywhere is a pre-teen boy, your age, who enjoys his sci-fi with a brunette villainess – a casting ploy you will protest, especially when you learn what will come next.

Each afternoon, without any adults to see, you re-enact an episode of the TV show V, alien lizards hiding in faux human uniformity. You are cast to play Diana, the dark-haired lizard queen, with some editorial enhancements, elementary- school obscene. The plot outlines are somewhat true, he writes it all down for you on blue-lined paper but the ending's changed, always a kiss at the end of the page. It's how you subdue the resistance each day, different male co-stars are written in the outline today to rebel and to challenge with words or a finger gun. The director decides which is the one.

You comply for a while though you know this is strange – a boy who wants you to kiss other boys for a change. Even this young, you know you are off the map, on a playground with a pervert, until one day you finally snap. You call him out with your own reptilian tongue, "I'm not doing it, geek," and you know the last word's stung as he approaches, his face increasingly red. You can't even believe this too-true mean thing you just said.

Before you can contemplate it one minute more, you whole body falls, folded over onto a treehouse floor, gasping and the cause is he punched you in the gut. Everyone's still, silent, mouths shut. Even the one whose fist you still feel, catching your breath, in a gingham dress, struggling to stand. He's too ashamed and afraid to approach or offer a hand. He's shaking with fright you are going to shake off this sand, run and spill the details of his crime – though you never will.

It's one of those things about you that many boys and men learn – predators over the years as they take their turn. Your dad's trained you well to keep it inside – the terrible things a girl shouldn't hide. You don't tell any teacher – very many friends. It will be high school before you speak to this boy again.

V IS FOR VIRGIN

Ever the director, you wrote the scripts
and cast the boys for me to kiss. Made me
a brunette evil Visitor, warm lips
belie her lizard heart and frigid sea
of blood that snakes inside. And you would know
because you read my thoughts on folded sheets
of blue-lined paper, stolen data showed
an alien desire, type cast to meet
those mouths you knew I craved. And I behaved,
your blacktop starlet, puckered lips you taught
to part on cue. A slipped, forked tongue you staved
with your first touch, a punch my stomach caught.
Still stuck inside these dramas that you made
concocted on a playground in fourth grade.

Suspicious of witches for centuries, you read the patriarchal takes in literature, the plays, the histories in school and on the library shelf. In reclusive Puritanical villainesses, you see yourself – deep in the woods, a Milleresque Abigail Williams, a teenager, stealth, dancing in a clearing without any clothes, half a mile in the center where almost nobody goes – never adults, sometimes boys with footballs or pot, illicit adolescent joys but more oftentimes not.

So while you take off your clothes in the afternoon sun, first skin, sinning in public, you spin, ears attuned to the sounds of the young – every crackle of leaves, small animal sounds goosebumps your flesh as you eyes shift around. Electric, the fear of discovery, the tingle of being seen being free.

You feel nakedly spiritual amidst a circle of trees; the way you never did in a chapel or on your knees. The embrace of the air sets every hair on end. You find your true nature while playing pretend – enacting a thing you read in a book. (One day, you will dance naked in public, and people will look.) Not today though, you'll hurry to slip back into clothes, suddenly aware, nervous you will be exposed and whipped by puritans you call your own. But you'll do it some more, when you're sure you're alone.

You'll check out all the books at the library about women defying the patriarchy with naked bodies, ingredients like boiled antennae and salt, aggregated to survive the organized misogynistic assaults. You become their familiar in the forest or in the library stacks; you are one more woman denied power, evolving, taking it back.

A CONFESSION ON A SALEM GALLOWS

(a sonnet by a teenage Kristin Garth)

"You have a faulty understanding of young girls. There is a promise made in any bed."
Arthur Miller, The Crucible

To Abigail, they say a ship has come
and gone like silver coins from uncles' chests.
For winter's here, and all you have undone
remains in soot. The amber blaze that tests
our common flesh has burnt its way past these
unrelinquished oceans to blushing lands
where we all swelter still in colonies
of misery, unchristian eyes and hands
that know no proper home. And though you sear
the very saints, it is our loss of warmth
that burns the most. Pointing fingers, we fear,
have stole the very sun. No smiles nor mirth
nor curling hair for me until I hang
and then will fly to you from death and rain.

Just some white paper, thumbnail-sized on the floor, you unfold, behold *I love you* before finally connecting it to *1984* – a tome you've been reading both at home, this high school English classroom – a succubus hiding inside a shy puritanical virgin costume. Often a skirt, inches below the knee, an expanse of wildflower fabric ironic over arms, to the neck, regardless of the southern humidity, modestly circumspect. You are a wildflower in a prim flower bed, purple from pruning, indistinguishable from dead.

From the living, unforgiving children, by clothes and customs, you are set apart in layers of fabric and your family's fundamentalist ways. You're sent, while kids snicker, to the school library on sex education days. Permission slips sent home, your parents, hot with moral outrage, were the only ones afraid to acknowledge teenage sexual activity, curiosity, developmentally appropriate lust of the young brain. A future Microsoft cloud developer, to your right, quiet, restrained, blue eyed teenage boy sees you blinking frustrated pleasure in pain, brown irises haughty with sublimated rage, peeking at him from inside your dystopian cage.

Like the one you've been reading, told with Orwellian flair, while you demurely make eye contact through brunette strands, untamable hair. (Your mom wanted to cut it down, like one day your own breasts; she suggests a plastic surgeon, until your father, unsurprisingly, protests). The hair, you stand firm, you won't budge or flinch; it's wild like your heart, and you protect each chestnut feral inch.

A mane thick with triumph and a frizzy dandelion sensuality, it's one of the unshameable parts of you a nerdy teenage boy sees and somehow understands. An Orwellian "ownlife" blinks its secret demands, he reads in iris flickers, he wants to hold in his hands. So he writes his declaration, throws it on the floor. You'll find an anonymous "I love you," not know who it was from or was for – but it will linger in thoughts as you finger tiny pencil script love in school; for three years he will think you rebuffed him and feel like a fool. But you just didn't know who this love belonged to, but in bed all alone, you touch, many nights, pretending it was you.

THERE'S HAZARD IN A HAPHAZARD LITERARY ALLUSION

In *1984*, she placed it in
his hand, a folded *i love you* note so he
might understand she was no Puritan
just camouflaged, Junior Anti-Sex League,

a survivalist sublimating need,
from hunters, terrified to bleed secrets
that some fifteen year old dark haired girl reads,
long skirt flirts with teen pervert, proximate,

unblinking eyes, English class, which surmise through
hemlines, hunched spine, a life not mine
dystopian heroine with curfew/
parents you hope folded paper undermines.

I'll find paper *i love you* on the floor —
touch, years, before I'll know who it was for.

You have a corseted curiosity, 18th century cleavage, a precocity you are forced to hide, like curves, inside an in ill-fitting homemade dress, opaque tights, bright white, to spite a would-be teenage temptress. It's a uniform you despise. Despite its hindrance, you see men's eyes always focused on your chest as if they see the underneath undressed.

Like the character Cecile Volange, in Dangerous Liaisons, your heart does not belong inside their corsets just yet but your body fits. Your childish beliefs you learn are counterfeit. Everyone tells you what to do. Adults say so many things untrue. Desires and observations no one wants to know; you remain, constrained prepared for show. It's not for you to argue with their ways. You are still their property and they will gaze.

Sometimes it is only trouble for you — your father's looks so many others see right through -- the few church girls your age allowed to spend the night, your mother who thinks it isn't right — not his attentions, your sinful shape no dress can repress. He can't escape. It's something their genetics did not give to you - you are an original through and through, a hedonist in a puritanical house, their curvy little schoolgirl mouse, who is allotted a pretty cage if you can be invisible and well-behaved - they could exterminate if it grows too depraved.

Sometimes it is only a joy. It might just be the neighbor boy, older by a couple of years but broad, blonde, bigger than your familial fears. He's the first boy you know who can drive — a golf cart only but you feel adult, alive in the passenger seat, wind against your hair, the chosen girl beside him there — scared your parents will come out and see, punish the iniquity of riding in a tiny car (a few streets away will feel so far) with a boy you wish would take to the highway for days. Neither of you with too much to say.

Giggling at kids racing behind, wanting a turn. He'll speed off until they are left far enough behind, spurned to park near the woods, to sit in silence and pines. He'll pull from a console a package of Red Vines. He'll never touch you just some stares and small talk of the mall, soccer balls. You chew and giggle, no words at all. But he makes this a ritual, pickup and drive away, a chauffeur again, another hour, some days. And, though, each time you are scared you'll be punished and caught, these drives feel like lessons, and you long to be taught.

ARE YOU NAIVE ENOUGH TO BE A WIFE?

for Pierre Choderlos de Laclos

Was wantonness weakened by a whalebone
cage? Did it waft from breasts exposed by stays?
Were gasps ecstatic, laced into a cone
of gold brocade, of girls around your age,
strategically displayed modest charms,
lithe arms in chintz — an innocence you must
always evince, of convent or a farm,
both unaware and unalarmed of just
how many eyes apprise what swells and cleaves,
your dress is formed to advertise? Perchance
to win a wealthy life. Are you naive
enough to be a wife — en manse, belle dance
in pageantry, piety, etiquette,
pretend no one yet has made you wet?

You will wait years past your peers before you can date. Even then, when you do, it feels like a miracle to you to be allowed in a car – to go away (not even that far) with a 17 year old boy, permissible joy. Your first date is as innocent as that slow incoming kiss. Eight years of maturation have imbued him with a new innocence

He was the boy who directed your playground lips to others his age until your unfortunate quip that sent him into a rage. He hit you, regretting it instantly. An elementary schoolfriendship ends but not irreparably

It will take over a handful of years. He'll grow sweeter and shy, quieter than his peers. In high school, he slowly begins to have small talk with you – asks lots of questions things you like to do. He wears a t-shirt one day that says your favorite show's name Twin Peaks. Suddenly, you have something about which to regularly speak

Speaking of Laura Palmer is easier than speaking about yourself. You like how in tune to her struggles he seems, his understanding of her mental health. Without ever saying it, you know it means he understands you. You don't have to explain it. He has been there and can see through ..

He was the boy who threw an *I love you* note on the floor – his haphazard allusion to 1984. He didn't think to put it in your hand – or maybe he was too shy, either way you did not understand he had come to love you over all of these years

Then eighteen, he asked you out, and the realization appears that he sat very close to you in English class, three years prior to his – you never thought to ask if this paper belonged to him – the paper you rubbed against your naked skin – without an idea it was written by him.

As his lips approach, you feel him shake. You have no fear of him any longer – for any childhood mistake. You know without having discussed it he's more and less experienced than you – consensually speaking, the physical, to you, is all new.

But you have been reading, finding your way – in the library, the last few years, and you're ready to play. You read so many books that teach you things about yourself you just didn't know. Just this year, you have read The Story of O ...

THE SECRET SOCIETY OF LAURA PALMERS

for Jennifer Lynch, author of The Secret Diary of Laura Palmer

Our fathers make us Lauras — yours with art,
                mine with his heart. We're their
     transcriptionists,
  the obscenities of seventeen, hearts
they halve, mine hidden, yours bidden by Lynch
himself to just "be Laura Palmer." Though
you are his own daughter, and 22,
somehow he knew you would imbue his show
    with orgiastic veracity. You
speak ripped page diary to me, small beach
town girl opened up some nights, spread leg fire,
deprived books, fingers, flashlights to be a piece
of demonology who he acquired
through genealogy to take apart.
Your father only used you for your art.

You find all kinds of erotica in the card catalogue – by seventeen you part of a private dialogue with writers of literature, smut and psychology, any medium which tackles sexuality. You seek them out by their subject. Some you cannot take home. Only the ones with plain covers, contents unknown to your conservative parents who fear bodies not books -- the most lewd one you hold against your chest without the slightest fear that your father protest.

It is The Story of O, a cream cover with a small conservative black type, no illustrations, subtitles, no theatrics or hype. It looks banal and foreign, to your parents neither interesting nor threat. They have no idea in this public library, it has made you wet.

You don't have a boyfriend and you haven't explored, but you begin on your own with this book on a library floor, reading its first pages again and again. They are full of penetrations and cocks and bodies whipped and exposed. There's rituals for service, rules for wearing stockings and clothes. It makes you quite dizzy the way it feels exactly like you.

To get to the end (in privacy) you know what you'll have to do – take it to the counter where there's only Ms. Rose. You'll have to be brave and completely composed, seventeen years old checking out porn from a woman who read you fairytales and made ornaments out of popcorn. A parental figure in your life who never beat you or controlled -- always spoke in a whisper, neither coerced nor cajoled, just taught you to seek self-knowledge liberally. Today feels like the ultimate test as you place it before her gingerly.

Afraid to make contact, afraid she'll finally say no, and what's inside these pages are things essential to know about a unique component of your sexuality. She's taught you to search here for answers confidentially. There is only a second a small shock she betrays as she looks at the cover then quickly away, back at you as she pulls out its card. Your heart is pounding as she stamps it with confidence, loud and hard then hands it to you the way she has thousands of times. She's smiling as usual, normal and kind,

And it occurs to you this is unconditional love – like your grandmother, the only family member these words make you think of. You take the books and wait for your dad to arrive. You don't even hide it from on the drive. He's not like Ms. Rose. He doesn't read. It's why he thinks libraries are safe – he doesn't need to monitor you here, to tell you what you can see. He thinks it is quiet and boring not licentious and free. Inside of these silent stacks, you are becoming exactly who you will be.

THE STORY OF SCARLET

for the teenage girl who found herself in the Story of O

Some day men will call you another name.
Some day some pay to put you on a plane.
Some stay in hotel suites where you are shamed.
Your name's a party password some obtain —
    riddle some hypothesize, explain
    the scarlet skin of one who entertains —
    etymology of dominant brains.
Truth? Taxonomist, teenage boy who trains
you, some day, to employ *Scarlet,* screename
of raven haired southern girls *Rhett* restrains,
for chatroom talks with ones who feel the same
    as you, college girl addicted to pain.
    It starts at 17, her knowing look,
    librarian, dirty library book.

PUBLICATIONS

Hot Pink was first published in *Tepid Autumn.*

A Library Card Is A License of the Mind was first published in *Punk Noir Magazine.*

Flower In Your Attic and *Clues* were first published in *Royal Rose Magazine.*

There's Hazard In A Haphazard Literary Allusion was first published by *8 Poems.*

Are You Naïve Enough To Be A Wife? was first published in *Petrichor Journal.*

V is for Virgin was first published in *Water Soup.*

The Secret Society of Laura Palmers was first published in *Impossible Task.*

Inside was first published in *Rag Queen Periodical.*

Kristin Garth writes as if her life depends on it. She is a genius in the deepest sense of the word, a wild yet exacting sonneteer. In *Dewy Decimals*, her gifts for rhythm and rhyme propel a scintillating story of sexuality and literature and their interconnectedness. These poems smolder on the page, then blossom in the mind as the poet comes into her own. Every word, every image, is earned. A powerful collection that is both liberating and a pleasure to read.
—Scott Neuffer, editor of *trampset*

Kristin Garth's "Dewy Decimals" is two sticky fingers holding place in a book, is a swan-dive into curious exploration, is a familiar, aching hunger for knowledge and for sex, is letting the mind wander in the margins of a beloved childhood book. Sometimes morbid, sometimes taboo, but also soft and relatable. This book is a pre-teen fever dream.
—Dani Tauber, author of *It's Always Summer in Hell* and *Baby's Breath*

"The sonnet form has always spoken back to past literature, walked on the dangerous terrains of love. Sonneteers are always haunted by books and lovers and Garth is at home among them. These poems remind us of what the long history of the sonnet was trying to do: reflect the boldest thoughts of a loving, aching, well-read mind at her highest brilliance. These are gems made by memory, perfected and tested by a skilled poet and master of the sonnet form."

Tim Duffy, PhD
Editor, *8 Poems*